Original title: Lost in the Horizon

Author: Aurelia Lende
Editor: Jessica Elisabeth Luik
ISBN 978-9916-39-972-9

Lost in the Horizon

Aurelia Lende

Final Gaze

In twilight's gentle fading light,
Shadows stretch and curtains rise,
A final glance towards the skies,
As day surrenders to the night.

The echoes of a distant past,
Whisper secrets soft and low,
In this moment, time moves slow,
And memories forever last.

Stars ignite the velvet dome,
Guiding dreams upon their way,
Each one holding silent sway,
A beacon for the hearts that roam.

Breath of wind and rustle leaves,
Nature's symphony unveiled,
In this peace, the soul exhaled,
And in the calm, the spirit grieves.

Eyes that glimpse the end of days,
Find solace in the twilight hue,
In the quiet, strength renews,
Within that sacred final gaze.

Dimming Distance

Twilight whispers soft adieus,
The horizon fades to gray,
Eyes trace the falling hues,
As night dissolves the day.

Mountains meld with the sky,
A canvas painted drear,
Distance dims and shadows lie,
Wrapped in evening's sphere.

Veils of dusk descend with grace,
Embracing earth in sleep,
Moonlight's glow takes their place,
In shadows, secrets keep.

Periphery of Night

Stars ignite the inky dome,
Along the edge of dreams,
On the fringe, where spirits roam,
Night's hush softly teems.

Voices whisper in the breeze,
Secrets dark and light,
Mingling through the ancient trees,
At the periphery of night.

Lunar beams and shadows dance,
In a serenade's soft flow,
Between realms, a fleeting chance,
Where night's mysteries grow.

Otherworldly Endings

Beneath the twilight's dim embrace,
A realm of echoes rise,
Where dreams and stars find their place,
In otherworldly skies.

Mystic winds through silence sweep,
Whispering tales untold,
In the void where shadows sleep,
Ancient truths unfold.

Transient as the falling snow,
Eternal as the sea,
Worlds where only dreamers go,
Endings wait to be.

Echoes of the Horizon

Beyond the edge where sky meets sea,
Whispers ride the waves,
Carrying secrets wild and free,
Through time's timeless caves.

Horizon echoes soft and clear,
In hues of dusk and dawn,
A symphony both far and near,
In twilight's gentle yawn.

Waves embrace the setting sun,
Kissing day goodbye,
Where echoes into night are spun,
Beneath a starlit sky.

Vanishing Verge

On the edge of twilight's seam,
Where fading dreams converge,
Shadows dance in silent gleam,
    At the vanishing verge.

Echos of the day and night,
    In whispers softly merge,
Moments lost in out of sight,
    At the vanishing verge.

Footprints in the sand erased,
    By time's eternal surge,
Memories both swift and traced,
    At the vanishing verge.

Oceans of Eternity

Waves that kiss the endless shore,
In depths of blue infinity,
Secrets held forevermore,
In oceans of eternity.

Sirens sing their haunting call,
Beneath the moon's serenity,
Tides that rise and gently fall,
In oceans of eternity.

Journeys long and currents deep,
In liquid vast fraternity,
Where dreams and mysteries sleep,
In oceans of eternity.

The Farthest Reach

Beyond the hills and valleys wide,
To where the world's contours beseech,
Lies a path untamed, untried,
To realms of the farthest reach.

Stars that beckon from afar,
Like dreams too wild to teach,
Every soul a wandering star,
In realms of the farthest reach.

Horizons dare the bold to stray,
Where wonders lie within arm's stretch,
Endless skies that call each day,
To realms of the farthest reach.

Nebulous Horizons

Through clouds of mist and mystic air,
Where sunrise melts and cryst, defines,
We wander forth without a care,
Towards nebulous horizons.

Colors blend in twilight's frame,
And swirl in softened lines,
Every dawn a whispered name,
Upon nebulous horizons.

Dreams unfold in shaded hues,
Where fate and time align,
Journeys new await to choose,
Beyond nebulous horizons.

Chasing the Distant Light

Through the darkened night, we roam,
Seeking stars, our distant home.
Every path, a woven thread,
Guides us where the dreams are spread.

Whispers in the moon's embrace,
Paint the hope on every face.
Traveling through the twilight's might,
Chasing dreams and distant light.

Voices call from future skies,
Far from where our present lies.
Hearts alight with fervent sight,
Onward to the dawning light.

Veiled Horizons

Beyond the mist, where shadows play,
Lies a world both bright and gray.
Mysteries in the misty seams,
Veiled horizons host our dreams.

Dreams take flight on wings unseen,
Painting skies of blue and green.
Softly whispered by the breeze,
Secrets held in silent seas.

Journeys start with hopeful eyes,
Crossing realms where magic lies.
Veiled horizons, yet so clear,
Shaping destinies we steer.

Quest Across the Horizon

With each dawn, our journey starts,
Boundless fields and endless charts.
Mountains tall, we rise and climb,
Spanning realms, defying time.

Ocean waves and starlit skies,
Where the heart's deep longing lies.
Every step, a story told,
Quest across horizons bold.

Paths entwined with boundless grace,
In the cosmic dance, we trace.
Ever questing, hearts ignite,
Guided by the celestial light.

Dancing With Shadows

Beneath the moon's soft, silken veil,
Shadows dance, their secrets pale.
Silent waltz on starlit floors,
Whispering of ancient lores.

Twilight's glow and dusky charms,
Lend a solace, soothe the harms.
Dreams entwine in shadowed beams,
Crafting stories, weaving dreams.

Flickering lights in twilight's frame,
Playing in the shadow's game.
Dancing with the night's embrace,
Finding peace in shadow's grace.

Glimmers on the Fringe

In twilight's grasp, where shadows dance,
A world begins its nightly trance.
Soft whispers float on evening's breeze,
As stars awake above the trees.

Glimmers on the fringe of night,
Guide the soul to seek the light.
Mysteries of dark unfold,
In stories ancient, softly told.

The moon—our lantern, silver bright,
Leads us through the velvet night.
Glimmers fade as dawn draws near,
Nighttime's secrets seem less clear.

Where the Day Sleeps

Where the day sleeps, the night ascends,
Upholding dreams time never ends.
Embrace in shadows, deep and true,
The sky reveals its darkish hue.

Soft lullabies, the stars impart,
To soothe the restless, weary heart.
In moon's soft glow, our worries fade,
As night weaves calm with tender shade.

Nature whispers in hush tones,
As midnight's magick softly hones.
In slumber's grasp, the world at peace,
Where daylight's burdens find release.

Edge of Infinity

On the edge of infinity's vast plain,
Questions linger, hopes remain.
Stars like beacons, endless in sight,
Pierce the blanket of the night.

Galaxies swirl in timeless dance,
Both chaos and a sweet romance.
Beyond the reach yet ever near,
A universe both wild and clear.

Infinite paths stretch wide and far,
Guided by a lone, brave star.
At the precipice, we gaze and dream,
Of worlds where endless wonders gleam.

Towards the Fading Gleam

As dusk embraces day's last hue,
We wander 'neath a sky of blue.
Towards the fading gleam we tread,
In fading light, the sky is red.

Shadows lengthen, stars appear,
Whispers build the night's frontier.
Beneath this cosmic, velvet dome,
Our thoughts like ships begin to roam.

In twilight's arms, our souls unfold,
In tales of wonder, softly told.
Towards the fading gleam we sail,
To where the night reveals its tale.

At the World's Rim

Silent whispers through the trees,
Where land and sky intertwine,
Mysteries float on the breeze,
Touching hearts with signs divine.

Waves crash upon the lonely shore,
Distant echoes of the past,
Stars no longer seen before,
In night's embrace their light will last.

Tales of old in twilight's gleam,
Anchored deep in souls that yearn,
Poets weave a timeless dream,
As the world begins to turn.

Ephemeral Glow

Candles flicker in the gloom,
Shadows dance along the walls,
Life's brief moments swiftly bloom,
With each rise and gentle fall.

Morning dew on petals bright,
Fades before the midday's shine,
Ephemeral glow of night's delight,
Lost in dawn's unfurling line.

Hold these moments soft and dear,
In the heart where they abide,
Transient beauty pure and clear,
Guides us on this fleeting ride.

Beyond the Setting Sun

Crimson shades paint sky and sea,
As the day bids soft farewell,
In the twilight's gentle plea,
Silent dreams commence to swell.

Journeys break upon the dusk,
Far horizons blend to one,
Mystic worlds of amber musk,
Lie beyond the setting sun.

Hope and memory converge,
Time's fleeting whispers blend,
In the shadows truths emerge,
As the night begins to mend.

Twilight's Reach

Golden embers kiss the land,
As daylight yields to night,
Twilight's reach, a gentle hand,
Guides the world with subtle might.

Stars begin their ancient watch,
Guardians of dreams untold,
In the silence shadows march,
Stories weave in threads of gold.

Nature hums a lullaby,
Ode to dusk's enchanting grace,
In the twilight, spirits fly,
Every heart in night's embrace.

Fading Boundaries

Across the lines that once confined
A world of colors, intertwined
No walls to mask the gentle breeze
Just open fields, where eyes can see

The borders melt in warm embrace
An endless dance, no need to chase
Horizons blend in twilight's hue
Where dreams and truth both bloom askew

In silent whispers, they dissolve
As spirits wander and evolve
From dawn to dusk, the paths renew
A journey shared by me and you

Lost in the echoes of the past
The shadows fade, the die is cast
Together, free of earthly bounds
In unity, our hearts resound

Wanderers of the Sky

Beneath the stars, we drift away
The night our guide, we soar and sway
Through constellations, vast and old
Our dreams are cast in cosmic gold

Eclipses mark our fleeting trails
As moonlight glimmers, tales unveil
Beyond the clouds, our spirits fly
As wanderers of endless sky

We trace the paths of comet's flight
And bathe in rays of satellite
In cosmic seas, we sail so free
With galaxies as company

Celestial veils we cast aside
In meteoric arcs, we ride
Bound not by earth, but by the light
Our journey spans eternal night

Beyond the Veil of Dawn

As night retreats, the dawn awakes
The sky adorned with amber flakes
Auroras paint the world anew
In shades of crimson, gold, and blue

The darkness fades, a glowing sea
Of endless light, our destiny
We sail beyond the morning veil
Where shadows wane, and dreams set sail

Through mists of time, our vision clears
The dawn reveals our hidden fears
Yet in its light, we find our way
To realms of hope by break of day

As morning dew collects and gleams
We rise, reborn from nightly dreams
In dawn's embrace, our souls ascend
To seek the truths that lie beyond

In the Wake of Dusk

As twilight breathes its final sigh
The stars emerge in night's soft cry
In shadows deep, the silence thrums
As dusk retreats, the evening hums

The world enclosed in velvet night
Where whispered dreams take silent flight
In twilight's shade, the soul may bask
In mysteries beneath its mask

The twilight's kiss on evening air
Unfolds the night, beyond compare
Embrace the calm, let spirits mend
In the wake of dusk, the night descends

The lanterns lit by starlight's gleam
Guide wanderers to realms unseen
In twilight's glow, new paths unfurl
As night begets the astral swirl

Journey into the Twilight

Softly fades the light of day,
Whispers of the dusk arise,
Shadows dance in gentle sway,
Twilight paints the evening skies.

Stars begin their quiet gleam,
Moonlit paths of silver trace,
In this realm of calm and dream,
Night enfolds us in its grace.

Whispering winds, a symphony,
Leaves that rustle, soft refrain,
In the twilight, wild and free,
Finds the soul its peace again.

On the Verge of Night

Crimson hues, the sky suspends,
Sunset's last and tender glow,
Day's embrace begins to end,
Night descends, a velvet show.

Starry punctures pierce the deep,
Chasing whispers of the light,
Veils of dusk, a silent sweep,
Creeping shadows blur the sight.

Time concedes to evening's lure,
Softly, gently, comes the night,
On the verge, where dreams are pure,
Darkness blooms to quiet light.

Fading into the Beyond

Soft the hues begin to whisper,
Daylight yields to twilight's kiss,
Shadows growing longer, crisper,
Fading softly into bliss.

Whirlwinds carry secret songs,
Beneath the stars, a cosmic play,
Life's narrative is gently longed,
As horizons melt away.

In the distance, echoes call,
Past the borders of the known,
Fading into twilight's thrall,
Where the soul may find its home.

Afterglow's Pursuit

In the afterglow's embrace,
Daylight's remnants softly cling,
Night approaches with its grace,
As the evening starts to sing.

Quiet murmurs fill the air,
Echos of the fading day,
In twilight's tender snare,
Light and darkness gently sway.

Chasing dreams in moonlit streams,
Boundless sky, a velvet chart,
In the afterglow's soft beams,
Night and soul are set apart.

Twilight's Reflection

The stars emerge in twilight's glow,
Soft whispers of the evening flow.
Shadows stretch across the land,
Night's quiet magic takes its stand.

The sky transforms to velvet night,
Where dreams and constellations light.
Gentle winds weave lullabies,
In monochrome, the beauty lies.

Moonlit ripples on the lake,
Dancing with each wave they make.
Serenity in every fold,
A tranquil tale in silver told.

Mountains silhouette the sky,
Dusk and dusk bid daylight bye.
Nature's mirror in the west,
Reflects the world's nocturnal rest.

Crossing into Ether

Whispers of the unseen air,
Guide us to realms beyond compare.
Mystic paths we tread with care,
Lost in dreams, so unaware.

Nebulae like silent words,
Float amidst the cosmic herds.
Timeless journeys in the night,
Through the dark, we search for light.

Galaxies in twinkling threads,
Span the skies above our heads.
Voyagers of the great expanse,
Led by fate, and chance, and glance.

Final call of distant shores,
Echoes past the astral doors.
In the ether, we find peace,
Boundless, weightless, soul's release.

Invisible Borders

Lines we draw, yet cannot see,
Define the 'you,' the 'they,' the 'we.'
In the heart where freedoms lie,
Borders fade and dreams can fly.

Mountains high and rivers wide,
Mark the paths where hearts divide.
Yet beneath a single sky,
Hopes and wishes unify.

Silent tales of lands unknown,
Sing the tune of seeds we've sown.
Bridging gaps with every thread,
Human tapestry widespread.

Kindred souls in foreign lands,
Join in peace with open hands.
Invisible, the lines dissolve,
In unity, our spirits evolve.

Nomad of the Heavens

Wanderer of the starry seas,
Roaming where the spirits please.
Galaxies in silent flight,
Guide the nomad through the night.

Beneath the glistening skies so vast,
Each step forward, from the past.
Seeking stories, truths untold,
Among the stars, the cosmos old.

Through the constellations' art,
Finds a place within the heart.
Eternal traveler, free and bold,
Wonders new and dreams unfold.

Meteors like whispers fly,
In the twilight's gentle sigh.
Heaven's nomad ever roves,
In the universe, the soul behoves.

Vanishing Point

The road ahead is endless
Where dreams and hopes align
Horizons blend to whispers
In twilight's soft design

Through shadows cast by daylight
And narrow paths untold
We chase the veiled illusions
As night begins to fold

The colors slowly blend in
An artist's hand unseen
The future glimmers softly
A place we've never been

Each step becomes ephemeral
Yet nothing feels amiss
We linger at the threshold
Entranced by transient bliss

With every breath a promise
In every glance a clue
The vanishing point beckons
To paths both old and new

Beyond the Skyline

A city bathed in twilight
Its secrets yet untold
The skyline whispers softly
Of stories brave and bold

Above the rooftops shadowed
Beneath a starry veil
Our dreams ascend in silence
On hope's unwritten trail

In every twinkling starlight
Is etched a distant goal
We venture forth undaunted
With passion in our soul

Beyond the iron structures
Beyond the earthly grind
Are tales of endless wonder
Awaiting those who find

So let us cross the threshold
Beyond the skyline bright
Into a world of mystery
And endless dreams alight

Whispers of the Unknown

In realms we cannot fathom
Lie whispers soft and low
Of ventures into mystery
Of places we don't know

Through shadows edged with silence
And caverns yet unclaimed
The whispers call us onward
Our spirits thus inflamed

The echoes of the ancients
In silent tongues they speak
Inviting us to wander
To find the truth we seek

Each step into the darkness
Is lit by faith alone
In realms of deep uncertainty
A path to call our own

For within the great unknown
Where mysteries unfold
Lie whispers of the future
And stories yet untold

Fading Sundown

The sun dips low in twilight
A symphony in gold
As day gives way to evening
New stories are retold

The sky transforms to canvas
Of hues both deep and bright
A fleeting work of beauty
That fades into the night

In shadows long and lengthened
We find a sense of peace
As day transcends to slumber
Our restless minds release

Each sunset holds a promise
In colors rich and deep
A whisper of tomorrow
As dreams begin to creep

In fading light, we ponder
On moments cherished dear
The sundown holds our secrets
Then vanishes from here

Spectral Shores

Whispers of waves on spectral shores,
Veil of mist, secrets it stores.
Halcyon hues under twilight's spell,
Echoes of time in the ocean's swell.

Footprints fade on silver sands,
Traces of myths in ancient lands.
Starlit arcs on the horizon gleam,
Wandering in an ethereal dream.

Phantoms dance where waters kiss,
Moments passed, eternal bliss.
Night's serenade to the moon in flight,
Shores that glow in the quiet night.

Silent tales by the briny crests,
Mariners' songs in peaceful rests.
Dreams dissolve like morning dew,
On spectral shores, old and new.

Edge of Beyond

At the edge of beyond, where stars convene,
Far from the realms of the known and seen.
Mysteries woven in a cosmic shroud,
Where silence reigns, majestic, proud.

Celestial paths through the inky expanse,
Eternal dance, a stellar romance.
Light-years stretch in an endless jest,
Time and space in infinite quest.

Lanterns of sky in the firmament's arch,
Guiding souls on a transcendent march.
Galaxies twirl in spirals grand,
Stories untold in the vast starland.

Parallel dreams in the spacetime weave,
All that is and can be perceived.
Edge of beyond, no boundaries known,
Ever-reaching, ever alone.

Chasing the Ever-Far

Through fields of gold and twilight haze,
Chasing dreams in the dwindling days.
Horizon beckons, a distant star,
On a journey to the ever-far.

Steps in rhythm with the whispering breeze,
Future's promise through the ancient trees.
Skyline shifts as the shadows play,
Guiding the soul on a boundless way.

Sunset hues in a painted sky,
Hope on wings as the moments fly.
Each heartbeat's pull to the unseen,
Tracing paths where fate has been.

In the quest for what's afar,
Reaching always beyond the bar.
Chasing moments swift and sweet,
In the journey, life complete.

Boundaryless Realm

In a realm without borders, vast and free,
Multitudes dance in grand decree.
No lines to bind, no chains to hold,
Tales of wonder in dreams retold.

Verdant plains stretch to skies unfurled,
Harmony reigns in this boundless world.
Echoes of laughter, joy unconfined,
Unity in diversity enshrined.

Winds that sing in harmonious rhyme,
Timeless tunes through the threads of time.
Nature's canvas, colors bleed,
In every heart a kindred seed.

Journeys weave through the endless plain,
Every soul, an everlasting gain.
Boundaryless realm where light does gleam,
Reality mirrors the wildest dream.

Horizon's Haunt

Upon the edge where sun meets sea,
Whispers of the past roam free,
Shadows dance in twilight's glow,
Echoes of what we may never know.

Waves crash against the rocky shore,
Tell tales of lands we can't explore,
Stars align in the evening hue,
Hearts wander where dreams construe.

Clouds drift in majestic ballet,
Marking the turn from night to day,
Mysteries in their fleeting form,
In silence, they weather the storm.

As dusk gives way to velvet night,
The horizon hides from sight,
Yet within, a spirit roams,
Seeking where the soul calls home.

Descent into Blue

In the depth of twilight's fall,
Where shadows stretch and spirits call,
The sky surrenders hues of red,
To the tranquil, deepening spread.

Nighttime dips in sapphire dreams,
Starlit echoes, silent seams,
As the world descends in peace,
Troubles find a sweet release.

Moonlit paths in gentle glow,
Guide the hearts that wander slow,
In this realm of midnight grace,
Worries fade without a trace.

Softly with the morning dew,
Whispers of the night renew,
Journeys end, yet still pursue,
The endless, boundless blue.

Mirage of Tomorrow

In the desert's endless sprawl,
A vision rises, clear yet small,
Future's breath in golden haze,
Promises of brighter days.

Oasis of what might be,
Dancing on the sands, set free,
Mirage speaks in whispered tones,
Hope stitched in ghostly stones.

Illusion of new dawn's birth,
Rise from this scorched earth,
In the glint of morning's light,
Emerges from the darkest night.

Seek the future, yet beware,
Fleeting visions in the air,
For in the mirage's glow,
The truth of tomorrow may show.

Bleeding Edge of Time

At the precipice of now,
Where past and future both endow,
Edges blur in temporal drift,
Moments pass, like sands they shift.

Time's horizon sharp and clear,
Fractures where the memories sear,
In the blood of yesteryear,
Echoes whisper what we fear.

Ticking clocks in silent halls,
Mock the fleeting hour's gall,
In this dance of light and dark,
Leaves on pages make their mark.

The present bleeds into what's next,
Scripted lines in fate's complex,
Yet within this fleeting shore,
We find the timeless evermore.

Elusive Day's End

As daylight whispers in retreat,
The gentle hues of twilight dance,
In soft embrace, where shadows meet,
A dreamlike, whispered romance.

The sun dips low, a golden flare,
A fleeting kiss upon the sea,
The night begins its tender care,
A lullaby of mystery.

Stars emerge, a sprightly choir,
Their melodies on silver strings,
In twilight's grasp, all hearts aspire,
And every soul finds gentle wings.

With every shade, the colors blend,
In harmony, the night descends,
Thus ends the race, the day's grand bend,
An elusive fate that never bends.

Silhouettes of Farewell

In the twilight's fading glow,
Shadows linger, soft and low,
Whispers of a day's sweet end,
As the night begins to blend.

Figures etched in twilight's hue,
Moments cherished, bold and true,
Soft goodbyes in the evening air,
Hearts entwined, beyond compare.

As the sunlight gently fades,
Memories in soft cascades,
Echoes of a day now passed,
In the night, our souls steadfast.

Moonlight casts a silver veil,
Over stories, old and frail,
In the night's embrace we dwell,
With silhouettes of farewell.

Ember Skies

Embers paint the evening sky,
Fiery hues that mesmerize,
A canvas rich with bold design,
As the day begins to die.

Flames of orange, strokes of gold,
A sight of splendor to behold,
The heavens blaze in warm array,
A tale of twilight softly told.

As dusk enfolds with gentle grace,
Softening the sky's embrace,
Stars emerge in quiet trance,
In ember skies, the night's advance.

Colors fade, but memories stay,
In twilight's soft and fleeting sway,
Ember skies, a fleeting show,
As day succumbs to night's soft glow.

The Final Glimmer

In the horizon's final gleam,
Daylight sighs its sweet farewell,
A tranquil pause in twilight's theme,
Where shadows rise, and daylight fell.

The final glimmer, soft and bright,
Ignites the sky with hues divine,
A moment caught 'tween day and night,
In every heart, a silent sign.

As the sun dips, a slow descent,
Night's soft whispers start to blend,
In quiet grace, the daylight spent,
An ending scene that we commend.

Stars awaken, one by one,
In the lingering glow of setting sun,
The final glimmer bids adieu,
As night prepares its grand debut.

Infinite Wanderings

Through the forests deep and green,
Where unseen shadows softly lean,
Whispers of the ancient pines,
Echoes of forgotten times.

Mountains kiss the sky's embrace,
Snow-capped peaks, a frozen grace,
Rivers carve their winding path,
A hymn to nature's aftermath.

Stars above in endless dance,
Glimmering with each night's chance,
Constellations stitch the night,
Guiding every wanderer's flight.

Desert's stretch, the sands of gold,
Secrets in the dunes unfold,
Beneath the sun's relentless gaze,
Mirages form in mystic haze.

Oceans vast, horizons wide,
Tides that ebb and flow with pride,
Every wave a brand new tale,
Infinite wanderings set sail.

Fleeting Frontier

Vast expanses yet unknown,
Territory seldom shown,
A fleeting frontier calls us forth,
Tales beyond our common North.

Sky meets earth in twilight hue,
Swapping shadows, different view,
Boundless realms and open skies,
Where ambition never dies.

Each sunrise a promised quest,
Adventure stirring in our chest,
Charting lands, sights unseen,
Chasing dreams in vibrant scenes.

Through the valleys, rivers wide,
Bound by spirit as our guide,
Endless is the path we tread,
Frontiers born with every step.

Horizon endless, always new,
Limitless, our vision too,
In every fleeting frontier find,
Stories timeless, intertwined.

Suppressing Daylight

Morning rays caress the dawn,
Night's illusions almost gone,
Yet shadows linger, day by day,
Suppressing light in stealthy play.

Clouds conceal the sunlit beams,
Masking all our hopes and dreams,
A battle waged 'twixt dark and bright,
In the grip of daylight's plight.

Curtains drawn to veil the glare,
Sheltered in the twilight's care,
Daylight fights to pierce the gloom,
Promising a brighter room.

Shadows stretch as hours fade,
Evening's cloak begins to wade,
And in this dance 'twixt night and day,
Light is born anew this way.

Whispers of a dawn suppressed,
In the silence, light confessed
Emerging through the darkest night,
Triumphant in the morning light.

Tales Untold

Whispers in the ancient halls,
Etchings on the crumbling walls,
Stories left unsaid, unknown,
In the shadows they have grown.

Pages yellowed, ink now faint,
Tales of heroes, sinners, saints,
Each a world left unexpressed,
Tales untold that never rest.

Songs unheard in silent airs,
Echoes of forgotten prayers,
Words that yearn to be released,
In the hushed of time they cease.

Parchment lost and letters burned,
Voiced once, now never turned,
Lives and legends, secrets hold,
Histories in tales untold.

Yet within these silent scrolls,
Linger dreams and aging souls,
Tales untold in quiet wait,
For the lips that speak their fate.

Following the Last Light

The sun dips low, a fading fire
Its embers spread across the sky
We've walked this path of dark attire
To chase the day, to say goodbye

The shadows lengthen, whispers pale
Soft echoes of the night unfold
We linger on this twilight trail
In search of warmth, in search of gold

The stars, they flicker into birth
A canvas strewn with silver bright
We meander through this dreamlike earth
Following the last light

With every step, the darkness grows
Yet still we press on, undeterred
In moonlit fields where silence flows
Each whispered thought, distinctly heard

As night embraces day's farewell
Our spirits soar, though dark surrounds
For deep within, our hearts will swell
Chasing horizons, endless bounds

Where Sky Meets Solitude

In endless blue, the clouds afloat
They drift with whispers of the unseen
A realm where dreams and silence coat
This place where doubts are washed clean

Horizons stretch, a silent vow
A promise kept by nature's grace
Where solitude and sky allow
A soul to find its hallowed place

The winds that weave through lofty heights
Bestow a calm that's seldom known
An endless dance in raptured flight
Where hearts and heavens are shown

The sun descends in gilded hues
A quiet peace pervades the air
Here solitude becomes our muse
In boundless sky, our souls lay bare

We find our truth beneath the dome
Where sky and solitude reside
This tranquil space we call our home
In endless reach, our hearts confide

Transcendent Twilight

As day gives way to twilight's glow
A symphony of shadows rise
Where time itself begins to slow
And daylight bids its goodbyes

The colors blend in hues unseen
A palette rich with promise held
In every stroke, a dream redeemed
In twilight's arms, our fears dispelled

Night's whispers float like gentle song
Through realms where mortal thoughts unwind
In twilight's grace, we find where we belong
A place where darkness intertwines

With light that dances, pure and fierce
Beyond the grasp of fleeting day
In twilight's hold, the veil it pierces
Transcendence claims its soft array

In quiet moments, we transcend
Through twilight's whisper, deep and wide
Where dreams and reality blend
In twilight's fold, we safely hide

Gazing at the Last Ray

The final beam of golden light
It stretches far, a tender sigh
In evening's arms, the day takes flight
And leaves a canvas, dark and shy

We gaze upon the fading line
A thread of warmth in cooling air
As night prepares to intertwine
Its velvet cloak with stars to share

Each ray a promise, softly spent
A moment's grace before the night
In gazing, silent hearts consent
To follow into peaceful light

The shadows cast in deep embrace
They whisper secrets of the past
As twilight falls with tender grace
We find reflections in the vast

In gazing at the last ray's glow
We touch eternity's soft stream
And in its light, our spirits grow
Infused with every twilight dream

Eclipsed Horizons

Once the sky wears a dim veil,
Stars begin their silent tale.
Ocean waves whisper dreams,
Under moon's silver beams.

Mountains stand in silhouette,
Secrets hidden, never met.
Wild winds through trees play,
Chasing shadows where they may.

Time dances to twilight's song,
Moments fleeting, never wrong.
Distant echoes, heartbeat's lure,
Of a world still unsure.

Eyes gaze upon the skies wide,
Magic woven, can't divide.
Horizons drawn by night's might,
Contours fading out of sight.

In the dark, horizons kiss,
Silent promises of bliss.
Eclipsed by night's gentle grace,
Beauty found in star's embrace.

Waning Light's Whisper

Golden hues grace the sky's edge,
Night approaches, makes a pledge.
Sun dips low, bids adieu,
Whispers secrets, to the few.

Trees adorned in shadows deep,
Crickets' choir, no time to sleep.
Leaves rustle with twilight's breath,
Nature's lullaby of death.

Sapphire skies turn to gray,
Stars align in their array.
Veil of night softly drapes,
Whispers through the starlit capes.

Embers of the day now fade,
Night's cool fingers, unafraid.
Luna rises, pale and bright,
Guides the stars' gentle light.

Through the quiet whispers sneak,
Soft and tender, secrets speak.
In the silence, night does grow,
Waning light its gentle show.

The Vanishing Point

Far beyond the reach of eyes,
Where the earth meets cloudy skies.
Horizons blend, lines dissolve,
Mysteries yet to resolve.

Paths converge and then diverge,
Souls in wander, on the verge.
Underneath the twilight's cloak,
Words unspoken, dreams provoke.

Moonlight casts a silver trail,
Through the night, where thoughts regale.
Echoes linger, whispering,
Silent truths, to shadows cling.

Steps that falter, others leap,
Into depths where secrets seep.
At the edge of what we know,
New frontiers, that gently glow.

In the distance, lines entwine,
Merging realms, the undefined.
Vanishing where worlds unite,
Bound by shade and bound by light.

On the Brink of Dusk

Evening settles, soft and low,
Sunset's final, gentle glow.
Birds cease their flight and call,
Nighttime spreads its quiet thrall.

Shadows stretch across the land,
Silent, peaceful, hand in hand.
Stars awaken, one by one,
Chasing glimpses of the sun.

Twilight's brush with hues so fine,
Paints the sky with lines divine.
Whispering leaves, the night's near,
Easing every latent fear.

Moon's ascent in quiet grace,
Light and darkness interlace.
Breaths grow steady, moments freeze,
Cradled in the evening's breeze.

On the brink where day does end,
Nighttime's secrets do extend.
Dusk's embrace, a gentle sigh,
Kisses earth and lights the sky.

Sunset's Epiphany

The sky is dyed in hues so bright,
A canvas painted by the night
Whispers of the day retreat,
In twilight's arms, the sun's defeat.

Golden glimmers, crimson seams,
A symphony of fading dreams
Mountains stand as shadows weave,
In quiet dusk, the heart believes.

Ribbons of a molten stream,
Drift through evening's gentle gleam
Silent echoes, moments cast,
In sunset's glow, time moves so fast.

The horizon bears a final light,
A lullaby for the approaching night
Epiphany in colors spun,
In silence, dusk and day are one.

A fleeting whisper, sunset's tale,
Ephemeral, yet ever so hale
In the closing, hearts align,
To ponder life's own grand design.

The Evaporating Line

Beneath the sky's expansive scroll,
Where dreams and shadows gently knoll
An unseen line begins to blur,
A boundary where truths confer.

In dawn's embrace, the night withdraws,
Clarity in nature's laws
Ephemeral, the line departs,
A whisper in the world of hearts.

The morning mist and dewy grass,
Meet where time and moments pass
Contours fade as light prevails,
A tale of ends and fresh travails.

Soft as breath, the edge dissolves,
Mysteries in light resolves
Transience in pure design,
Life perpetuates this line.

In vapor trails of what has been,
Lies the essence of the scene
Ephemeral this boundary's stay,
Evolving with the break of day.

Celestial Brink

Above the world, a velvet sea,
Where stars are galaxies' decree
A tranquil edge of cosmic flight,
Illuminates the endless night.

The moon, a sentinel so high,
Keeps watchful gaze upon the sky
Planets spin in silent grace,
Distant dreams in charcoal lace.

Swirls of galaxies afar,
Speak whispers of the astral spar
Infinite, the deep expanse,
A symphony of chance and dance.

Celestial brink, where dreams ignite,
Immortalized in starlit light
Infinite shores of wonder gleam,
In the tapestry of cosmic dream.

Eons pass, yet stars endure,
A testament to all that's pure
Boundless realms, uncharted space,
In celestial brink, we find our place.

Distant Veil

Beyond the hills, a misty shroud,
A phantom in the twilight crowd
An echo of the world's embrace,
A veil that hides a distant place.

Silhouettes in twilight flit,
Mysteries in shadows knit
Between the realms of seen and feel,
A border where the senses reel.

In the haze of morning's birth,
Emerges the veil's ghostly mirth
What it holds, none can be sure,
Secrets wrapped in twilight's blur.

The veil recedes with warming rays,
Unveiling truths of yesterdays
Ephemeral, its fleeting stay,
Dissolving in the light of day.

Yet as night returns once more,
The veil descends, as before
A reminder of the realms unseen,
Of dreams that lie in twilight's sheen.

Boundless Chasm

A gape that swallows endless light,
Reflects the void, an endless night,
Whispers echo through its breath,
A chasm wide, a leap of faith.

Eyes peer deep into the mist,
Darkness holds a cold, tight fist,
Stars above seem miles away,
In this boundless chasm, we sway.

Hope clings tight to fragile seams,
Dreams intertwine with shadowed dreams,
Infinity, a daunting brink,
Where thoughts and fears begin to sink.

Ledges mark our faintest tread,
Silent voices, long since fled,
Abyssal heart that knows no end,
Boundless chasm, my somber friend.

Illusions shift, reality blurs,
Ancient secrets, it confers,
Infinite stretch of dark and deep,
A boundless chasm where shadows creep.

Brink of Desolation

At the edge of the world's despair,
Echoes faint, and silence rare,
Lonely hearts and empty skies,
Desolation's bitter cries.

Winds that whisper cold and dry,
Forgotten hopes, a silent sigh,
With every step, the ground betrays,
On desolation's edge, we gaze.

Desert sands and barren trees,
Tales of sorrow carried by the breeze,
Ruins stand as time's old scars,
Underneath the watching stars.

Shadowed paths where none have tread,
In this place where dreams have fled,
Aching void where once was bright,
Desolation's endless night.

Tears can only carve the stone,
In a world so cold, alone,
On the brink, our hearts lay bare,
Desolation's whispered prayer.

Ghosts of the Horizon

Silent phantoms shift and glide,
At the brink where worlds collide,
Horizon's edge, where dreams do fade,
Ghosts of twilight, softly swayed.

Whispers carried on the breeze,
Echoes of forgotten seas,
Shapes that dance in fading light,
Specters of the waning night.

Lost in time, they wander free,
Veils that blur their frail decree,
Ghostly forms on shadow's crest,
In horizon's arms, they rest.

Dim and ghostly, past they trace,
Hands that linger, soft embrace,
In the twilight's gentle hue,
Phantoms cradle dreams anew.

Far they stretch, horizon's line,
Silent whispers, soft design,
Ethereal, yet close they stand,
Ghosts of horizon's twilight land.

Deserted Outlines

Traces left in shifting sands,
Echoes of forgotten lands,
Empty paths where shadows play,
Deserted outlines slowly sway.

Cactus guards the silent scene,
Where the winds of time convene,
Outlines fading, cracked and dry,
Underneath the cobalt sky.

Forsaken tracks of memories,
Haunted by the silent breeze,
Footprints lost in dust and time,
Desert's harsh and endless rhyme.

Mirage of life that once did bloom,
Swallowed by the sand's dark plume,
Outlines linger, faint and grim,
Underneath the twilight dim.

Shapes that mark a bygone day,
Dissolve with each sun's dying ray,
Deserted, yet they softly shine,
In the desert's drawn outline.

The Distant Glow

In the quiet night, a distant glow
Whispers tales of far-off lands
Where dreams are free to ebb and flow
And time slips softly from our hands

A golden thread through velvet skies
Binds our hearts to stars unknown
Illuminates where shadow lies
With secrets of a world half-shown

In glistening beams, we place our hopes
A gentle light in dark expanse
Through life's ever-winding slopes
We follow in a moonlit trance

The silent glow, a beacon true
Guides lost souls with soft caress
In its warmth, we are renewed
Bound by light, we find our rest

As night surrenders to the dawn
Memories of light remain
A silent echo carried on
Until the stars return again

Beyond the Twilight Path

Shadows stretch as dusk descends
Along the twilight's winding path
Where time, like mist, so subtly bends
To welcome evening's tranquil bath

Here, silence speaks in whispered tones
Of journeys yet to be unveiled
Where weary hearts find resting thrones
And whisper secrets once impaled

Beyond the glow of fading sun
A world awakening to dreams
Where night adventures have begun
Casting stars in cosmic streams

Through this passage, souls embark
On quests beneath the silvered sky
Led by light and cloaked in dark
To realms where whispers never die

In twilight's grasp, we find our peace
A path that leads to calm and grace
Where heartbeats of the night increase
And stars outline love's vast embrace

Glimmer at the Edge

At the horizon's shimmering line
A glimmer hints at stories grand
Of lands where stardust intertwines
With every wave upon the sand

Where twilight meets the ocean's breath
A hidden world begins to glisten
Life's whispers float, defying death
Inviting hearts to pause and listen

A spark of hope, a fleeting light
Guides the lost and wishful souls
Promises kept within the night
Lead them to their destined goals

Glimmers dance on water's edge
Like whispers in the evening's ear
They hold the power of a pledge
To chase away the darkest fear

When daybreak tears the veiled dark
A trace of night remains below
A promise kept, an unclaimed mark
A glimmer's truth we'll seek to know

Edge of Infinity

On the precipice of night and day
Infinity spreads before our eyes
The edge where dreams and stars hold sway
Unfolding stories, endless skies

Here, galaxies begin to swirl
In cosmic dance of light and time
Where mysteries of the stars unfurl
And souls embark on paths sublime

The vast expanse, a boundless sea
Of wonders yet to be revealed
Where hearts and minds can wander free
And all the cosmos is unsealed

At this juncture, space and thought
Combine in spirals of delight
Through every lesson life has taught
We glimpse the universe's height

Standing on infinity's brink
We find our place amid the stars
In awe, with every breath, we drink
Of timeless beauty, ours and Mars

Eclipsing the Day

Shadows dance in fleeting gray,
Moon's embrace on sunny ray.
Silent whispers, night's ballet,
Eclipsing the bright display.

Stars align, a cosmic play,
Daylight drifts, a muted fray.
Unseen paths in twilight lay,
Nature's veil in soft array.

Silent skies in still array,
Dreams unfold in dusk's bouquet.
Celestial secrets, hidden way,
Underneath the night's foray.

Twilight calls, the sun's decay,
Mystic hues on skies of clay.
Moments blend in soft relay,
Eclipsing all that's bright and gay.

Darkness blooms where shadows stay,
Moonlit threads in silver stray.
Gentle night, its muted sway,
Eclipsing shadows of the day.

Uncharted Ends

Voyage through the unknown sea,
Waves that whisper, wild and free.
Maps uncharted, destiny,
Guides us to our mystery.

Stars above in twilight gleam,
Illuminating dreams that seam.
Journeys written in a stream,
Beyond the edge, a distant theme.

Wander far where oceans blend,
Horizon's call, where doubts suspend.
Every curve and journey send,
To uncharted fates ascend.

Nature's compass, winds that lend,
Paths of wonder, hearts to mend.
Unknown shores as twilight bend,
Charting realms where tales extend.

Endless quests where twilight mend,
Journeys new, new paths to tend.
Every point a cosmic trend,
To uncharted worlds, our sails extend.

Pursuing the Pale Light

Through the mist, a beacon glows,
Guiding where the shadow flows.
Soft and pale, the light still grows,
Beckoning where no one knows.

Veiled secrets in twilight shows,
Hope afar in tender throws.
Silent dreams in night repose,
Pursuing light through quiet rows.

In the dark, a glimmer goes,
Leading hearts through gentle lows.
Pathways wrapped in hidden woes,
Follow light through whispered blows.

Mystic beams in night bestows,
Pale glow where the twilight slows.
Sacred steps in moonlit prose,
Pursuing light where no one goes.

Soft and pale, the beacon bows,
Tracing paths as night allows.
Luminescent dreams enclose,
Pursuing light as twilight sows.

Waning Worldview

Once a world in vibrant hue,
Colors shift, becoming few.
Changing tides, perspectives new,
Shaping what's held true to view.

Sunsets glaze in amber hue,
Moments fade in subtle cue.
Night approaches, shadows grew,
Waning light in evening's dew.

Boundless skies turn into blue,
Stars awake in night's accrue.
Reality shifts, a cosmic stew,
Waning light brings thoughts askew.

Vision blurs as dusk ensue,
Mysteries in twilight grew.
Reflections form a mirrored clue,
Waning light in shrouds of blue.

Once was bright now tinged with rue,
Perception shifts, an altered slew.
As night unfolds its silent cue,
Waning light, our world anew.

Journey to the Beyond

Upon the twilight's fading gleam,
We venture towards a distant dream.
Stars alight, our guide it seems,
Through endless night, on astral streams.

Oceans whisper tales untold,
Mountains glow with secrets old.
Time dissolves in cosmic fold,
This journey deep, our courage bold.

Spirits call from realms afar,
Lighting paths like morning star.
No boundary, no earthly bar,
In this voyage, bizarre.

Whispers of the past do fade,
Future's light, a new cascade.
Across the void, where shadows wade,
In the beyond, our souls displayed.

Embrace the unknown, do not fear,
For every end brings something near.
Journeys taken hold us dear,
In distant lands, we shall revere.

Slipping Beyond Sight

Through mist and shadow, we proceed,
On secrets dark, our hearts do feed.
Horizons blur, our eyes recede,
In twilight's grasp, our souls decreed.

Dreams unfurl in spectral light,
Guiding us through endless night.
Memories fade, and spirits take flight,
Slipping softly out of sight.

Voices call from distant shores,
Echoes of forgotten wars.
In silence, truth restores,
The passage to unseen doors.

Shadows dance in moonlight's sheen,
Life and death meet in between.
Through the veil so thin and keen,
We dissolve in the unseen.

Hearts align with cosmic rhyme,
Binding threads beyond all time.
In serenity, we climb,
Where mortal eyes see not the prime.

Golden Brink

At the edge of morning's rise,
Where dawn embarks on golden skies.
Horizons blend, a sweet surprise,
In this realm, no secret lies.

Fields of amber, oceans blue,
Eternal calm, forever true.
Natures song, a gentle coo,
On the brink, we start anew.

Breezes carry whispers old,
Of tales and dreams in hearts they hold.
Warmth of sun, no fear, no cold,
In golden light, our fates unfold.

Mountains blend with heavens near,
Boundless beauty, pure and clear.
Steps we take without a fear,
To golden brink, where souls adhere.

Hopes converge, and sorrows cease,
In this place of endless peace.
Heart and mind in sweet release,
On golden brink, life's masterpiece.

Pathway to No Return

On this road of fleeting sand,
Footsteps wash from shifting land.
Each step forward, worlds expand,
Pathway to the no man's land.

Beyond the bend where shadows fall,
Silent calls no echo stall.
Through the threshold, standing tall,
Into the infinite, heed the call.

Winds of change blow ever strong,
Guiding us, where we belong.
In emptiness, a distant song,
To the unknown, we move along.

Time's illusion fades away,
Night dissolves in dawning day.
Journey's end, come what may,
In no return, we're here to stay.

Souls traverse what once they yearned,
In lessons learned and bridges burned.
Infinite path, forever turned,
Onwards through the no return.

Outskirts of Dawn

A whisper of light in morning's cocoon,
Glimmers of gold in the dew-kissed air.
The sky bursts forth from night's maroon,
Revealing a world bright and fair.

Mountains stretched, their summits gleam,
While rivers flow with silent grace.
Nature awakens from a dream,
In dawn's tender, warm embrace.

Birds alight with joyous song,
Their melodies a call to rise.
Silence breaks, and joins the throng,
As sunlight paints the open skies.

Shadows flee from light's advance,
Day begins its slow unfurl.
Life resumes its endless dance,
On the outskirts of a waking world.

Yet in this brief, enchanted span,
Promise whispers, hushed and drawn.
For in the heart of every man,
Lies hope reborn at break of dawn.

Glimpsing Beyond

A curtain drawn, a veiled expanse,
An echo drifts from worlds unseen.
In shadows cast by happenstance,
Lie secrets cloaked in twilight sheen.

Through fractured light and mirrored mist,
Truths elusive, softly call.
In every shadow, dreams persist,
In visions grand, though often small.

To glimpse beyond, to dare to see,
What lies beneath the surface calm.
The mind embarks on journeys free,
With heartbeats loud, a pulsing balm.

The universe, a silent guide,
Hints at realms beyond our view.
In fleeting moments, we confide,
As wonders old become anew.

So seek the glimpse and chase the spark,
Within the depths of thought and soul.
For in each shadow hides a mark,
Of wisdom's light that makes us whole.

Twilight's Threshold

At twilight's edge, where day meets night,
The sky is painted, hues of fire.
A fleeting dance of waning light,
Invokes the spirit's deep desire.

The sun descends in soft retreat,
While stars ignite the velvet dome.
In twilight's arms, the worlds compete,
As night prepares to claim its throne.

Whispers float on evening's breeze,
As shadows stretch and stories weave.
The air is filled with silent pleas,
Of secrets dusk intends to leave.

Time stands still at twilight's gate,
Where boundaries fade and moments blend.
Embrace the magic, contemplate,
This transient phase where dreams extend.

For in this space of in-between,
Lies beauty, pure and undefined.
In twilight's glow, our hearts convene,
And glimpse the truth where thoughts unwind.

The Great Divide

Between the worlds of here and there,
A chasm wide, profound and deep.
A boundary drawn in subtle air,
Where secrets lost in silence keep.

Bridges form of hope and trust,
To span the gap between our minds.
Yet fragile as the thinnest dust,
These connections time unwinds.

We wander close to edges steep,
On precipices bold and grand.
Peering into shadows' sweep,
With eager heart and trembling hand.

The great divide, a test of will,
A journey fraught with doubt and fear.
Yet crossing over, hearts stand still,
As unity brings vision clear.

So dreamers leap and rise above,
The canyons' grasp, the endless night.
For in the end, it's faith and love,
That turn the dark to guiding light.

Whispers Beyond the Edge

In shadows cast by twilight's shade,
The whispers sing of dreams delayed,
A murmur soft, a ghostly thread,
Of worlds beyond the life we led.

The echoes call from yonder skies,
With secrets hid from human eyes,
A world unseen, yet deeply felt,
Where bygone hopes and sorrows melt.

The edges blur 'tween night and day,
As whispers guide the hearts astray,
To realms where time and space converge,
In spectral whispers, thoughts emerge.

Beyond the edge, a whisper's grace,
In silence found, an endless chase,
Where shadows meet the dawning glow,
And secrets of the heart bestow.

Through whispers faint and whispers clear,
A journey fraught with dread and cheer,
To realms unknown, just past the verge,
Where whispers shape the dreams they urge.

Chasing Vanished Suns

Through skies where fleeting shadows run,
We chase the light of vanished suns,
In twilight's grip, the darkness fades,
While memories like light parades.

With every dawn, a chapter turns,
As eager hearts and spirits yearn,
To grasp the glow of yester-light,
And wander mid the falling night.

In every breath, a silver trace,
Of fading dreams etched on the face,
Where vanished suns and glories past,
In whispers of the night, they last.

Yet dawn shall rise, and suns reborn,
Shall guide our souls through veils forlorn,
Until the echoes finally cease,
And grant our restless hearts their peace.

Amid the chase, 'neath starlit shroud,
We find the strength to stand unbowed,
For suns may set, and dreams may wane,
But hope shall ever rise again.

Eclipsed by Distance

Across the miles, a silence grows,
As distant stars in velvet rows,
Our hearts once close, now far apart,
Eclipsed by distance, aching hearts.

The letters fade, the words collide,
Emotions lost on moonbeam tides,
A chasm wide, a shadow cast,
By distance wrought, a love surpassed.

Yet in the dark, a beacon's gleam,
The memories of our shared dream,
Though distance reigns, the echoes play,
In whispered thoughts, we find our way.

Through nights alone, the heart still yearns,
For times where love and fire burned,
Though distance dims our eyes with tears,
Our love transcends the distant years.

So know, my love, though far you be,
In dreams we sail a boundless sea,
Eclipsed by distance, hearts confined,
Yet in each beat, our souls entwined.

Twilight's Vanishing Line

In twilight's calm, where day departs,
The vanishing line enshrines our hearts,
A fleeting wisp of golden hue,
Where night encroaches in deep blue.

The shadows lengthen, stars ignite,
A silent dance 'twixt dark and light,
Where boundaries fade, the worlds entwine,
Upon twilight's vanishing line.

In whispered breeze, the secrets hide,
Of realms unseen, on shadow's tide,
Where dreams are etched on twilight's seam,
In twilight's breath, we gently dream.

The fading light, a silent vow,
That dawn shall pierce the night somehow,
But in this space, 'twixt dusk and morn,
A world unique is softly born.

So take my hand, and journey near,
Where twilight's line dispels our fear,
In twilight's vanishing embrace,
We find our hearts and shared grace.

Vagabond's Peak

In wandering shoes, we seek the crest,
Through forest whisper, our quest expressed.
The moon's a lamp, the stars our guide,
On this rough trail, where dreams reside.

Each step a tale, both old and new,
The path we carve, beneath sky's blue.
Mountains echo our silent prayer,
To reach the peak, the journey fair.

With hearts afire and spirits wild,
We climb like youth, so free and mild.
The wind's embrace our only cloak,
In nature's arms, we find our hope.

Sunrise paints the morning bright,
Endless visions in purest light.
The summit calls, its voice so clear,
Vagabonds rise, we have no fear.

In fleeting moments, we stand tall,
Witness to the world, to beauty's call.
A vagabond's dream upon that peak,
To wander free, the world we seek.

Hem of Day

The dawn's first light softens the sky,
Night's last whisper bids goodbye.
Morning awakes with a tender grace,
Caressing earth with a warm embrace.

Shadows flee at the sun's command,
Daylight spreads across the land.
Birds proclaim the rise of day,
In melodies that gently sway.

Petals open to greet the morn,
In fields of gold, the new day's born.
With every ray, a promise near,
The hem of day, so bright and clear.

Woodlands stir with rustling leaves,
A symphony the dawn achieves.
Soft and pure, the breezes play,
In nature's realm, we find our way.

As time unfolds, the journey starts,
With hope embedded in our hearts.
From rise to set, the hours convey,
The woven thread of a perfect day.

Falling Daybreak

Morning spills from night's embrace,
Glimmers of gold, a silent grace.
Softly stretching across the fields,
A promise of light, the dawn reveals.

Each leaf kissed by gentle rays,
Awakening in newfound ways.
Nature's breath, an early sigh,
As colors bloom under the sky.

Mist retreats, to shadows' end,
A fleeting dance, as night suspends.
Birdsong pierces the quiet air,
With melodies both bright and fair.

Mountains greet the rising sun,
New beginnings, day's begun.
Upon the breeze, whispers fly,
Of stories old, and dreams nearby.

In the canvas of morning light,
We find our path, in colors bright.
Falling daybreak, softly sings,
A fresh new world that morning brings.

Cloudline Dreams

High above where earth meets sky,
Dreams ascend, and time slips by.
Whispers ride the winds so free,
In cloudline realms, our minds can see.

Soft and fair, the clouds do drift,
In their arms, our souls uplift.
Imagination's boundless flight,
Soars beyond the day and night.

Sunlight weaves through patterns white,
Creating visions soft, yet bright.
With every breeze, the dreams reshape,
A dance of light, a graceful drape.

Horizons broaden, endless blue,
In heaven's vast and gentle hue.
We chase the dreams that clouds portray,
In skyward peace, we find our way.

Through endless skies and lofty themes,
We wander soft in cloudline dreams.
In altitude, our spirits rise,
To touch the stars, beyond the skies.

Celestial Divide

Stars ablaze in velvet night
Galaxies in endless flight
Moon and sun, a dance so grand
In vast cosmos, shadows stand

Planets spin on axis known
Constellations brightly shown
Light and dark in cosmic play
Balance reigns in night and day

Comets weave through stellar webs
Mystic paths, their tales they shed
Auroras paint the skies with light
A divine and splendid sight

Nebulas, in hues so bold
Stories of the past unfold
In the silence of the space
Endless wonders to embrace

From the macro to minute
In the vastness, absolute
Mysteries that guide our quest
In the ether, hearts find rest

Ebb and Horizon

Waves that kiss the sandy shore
Whispers of the ocean's roar
Morning sun in colors bright
Heralds of approaching light

Tides that ebb and gently flow
Hide the secrets down below
Creatures dance beneath the waves
In the deep, where sunlight braves

Horizon caught in dreamer's gaze
Promises of distant days
Ships that venture far from home
Endless seas where dreamers roam

Twilight paints the sky with gold
Stories of the sea retold
Stars emerge as night takes hold
Calming tales of sailors bold

In the silence of the night
Moon on water, softly bright
Ocean's breath, a lullaby
To the dreaming, restful sigh

Shadowed Crest

Mountains rise with jagged peaks
Silent guardians that nature seeks
Shadows stretch as daylight fades
Nighttime slowly invades

Winds that whisper through the pines
Ancient tales and olden lines
Nature's secrets, deeply veiled
In the silence, softly hailed

Valleys bathed in twilight's glow
Whispers of the past they show
Ridges dark where light won't crest
Nature's majesty confessed

Owl's call through shadowed trees
Echoed in the midnight breeze
Creatures stir in hidden nests
In the forest's secret quests

Moon ascends, a silver crown
On the crests of mountains, brown
Stars above in silent vow
Watch the world from heights so proud

Ephemeral Line

Moments fleeting, swift as breeze
Time that whispers through the trees
Seconds slip through grasping hand
In the shifting, sinking sand

Dewdrops fade with morning sun
Life's great race that's never won
Ephemeral as morning mist
Memory's grasp in fleeting twist

Day and night in endless chase
World spins on in fateful race
Moments gone before we know
In their wake, the memories show

Love and laughter, fleeting sweet
Footsteps gone from ancient streets
Ephemeral, our line we trace
In the vast and timeless space

Cherish now, in present hold
Glimpse of beauty, bright and bold
Life's brief dance in fleeting time
Precious, fragile, yet divine

Sunset's Last Embrace

In the amber glow of twilight's lace,
The day bows out with gentle grace.
Hues of gold and blush unfold,
A tale in colors softly told.

Waves whisper secrets to the sky,
As stars prepare to wink on high.
Moments linger, hearts converge,
In sunset's arms, worries purge.

Shadows stretch across the land,
Night and day hand in hand.
Silent vows the horizon keeps,
As the world softly sleeps.

Nature's canvas, a fleeting sight,
Transitions softly into night.
Peace descends, a hushed embrace,
In the sunset's gentle chase.

In this stillness, time suspends,
Where daylight's journey ends.
A masterpiece in hues and shades,
As twilight's beauty fades.

Dreams on the Periphery

Whispers of dreams dance on the edge,
Of conscious thought, a silver thread.
Softly weaving night's abode,
In twilight's transient code.

Wishes ride on moonbeam streams,
Carried by the quiet of dreams.
Where fantasies gently stir,
In shadows deep, yet pure.

Glimpses of the unreal swirl,
In the quiet night, they unfurl.
Vague shapes of a thousand flights,
Through the velvet of the nights.

The mind rides on gentle tides,
To lands where imagination hides.
Each breath a key to unknown doors,
In the realm where the spirit soars.

On the periphery, dreams entwine,
With the silent march of time.
Echoes of tomorrow found,
In night's soft, enchanted sound.

The Faraway Line

On the horizon, distant and fine,
Lies the faraway, endless line.
A meeting point of earth and sky,
Where dreams take wing and softly fly.

Beyond the reach of grounded feet,
A place where time and silence meet.
Vista blurred, yet crystal clear,
A beacon to the hearts that steer.

Journeys borne on winds of hope,
Nurtured by each gentle slope.
The distant call that whispers nigh,
Where aspirations fly high.

The line that stretches out in grace,
Guides each soul in its embrace.
A compass in the vast unknown,
Where dreams and destinies are sown.

In the faraway, we chase the light,
A pursuit through day and night.
Ever drawn to the horizon's tease,
To the line that never ceases to please.

Pursuing the Unseen

In the shadows where dreams reside,
Lies a world where hopes divide.
Chasing whispers, unseen threads,
Through the labyrinth in our heads.

Fleeting forms and phantom lights,
Guide us through the endless nights.
Invisible to the waking eye,
Yet vivid 'neath the crescent sky.

Seeking paths that lie in mist,
In pursuit of what the heart insists.
Every echo, a guiding star,
In a journey near yet ever far.

Through the void, our spirits chase,
The unseen beauty, a silent grace.
Each step closer to the unknown,
In the quest for truths unshown.

Unseen realms we strive to see,
Bound by dreams and destiny.
With every heartbeat, every sigh,
We chase the stars across the sky.

Limitless Boundaries

Beyond the hills, where skies expand,
A world unfurls, untouched by hand.
Dreams take flight, on whispering breeze,
In realms of thought, time's tendrils tease.

Stars align in cosmic dance,
With endless chance, in life's expanse.
Horizons wide, no end in sight,
In boundless space, hearts find their light.

Beyond the reach of earthly chains,
Freedom reigns, where spirit reigns.
Through clouds we soar, to worlds anew,
In search of truths, both old and true.

Mountains rise and valleys fall,
In nature's grand, eternal sprawl.
Unseen paths and hidden ways,
Each step a dance, in cosmic plays.

Limitless, yet gently bound,
In silent whispers lost and found.
Infinity in moments brief,
A tapestry of joy and grief.

Ephemeral Dusk

The sun descends, with tender glow,
As shadows stretch, where night will grow.
A fleeting time, 'tween day and night,
A gentle kiss of fading light.

Whispers soft in twilight's grasp,
Moments linger, then they lapse.
Colors blend in silent hue,
A canvas brief, yet ever true.

In dusk's embrace, the world stands still,
Silent murmurs, whispering thrill.
Stars awaken, one by one,
Their journey starts as day is done.

Softened edges, blurred and kind,
In this light, we ease our mind.
A transient dance of dark and bright,
Ephemeral dusk, gives way to night.

The veil descends, the quiet reigns,
Night's calm comfort, still remains.
In the heart of twilight's glow,
Eternal peace, our spirits know.

Secrets of the Dawn

Morning whispers, soft and clear,
Secrets held, so near, so dear.
A breath of new, in light's embrace,
Awakening life with gentle pace.

Dew-kissed blooms and silent streams,
Hold stories wrapped in morning beams.
In dawn's first light, the mysteries play,
Hints of dreams in break of day.

Birdsong weaves through morning mist,
Songs of love, of light's first kiss.
Nature's chorus, heart's delight,
In dawn's embrace, fades the night.

Mountains high and valleys deep,
Secrets in their shadows keep.
First light's touch, reveals the veils,
Tales untold in dawn's sweet trails.

Golden hues on morning's breath,
Whispers soft as night's last death.
In dawn we find, new stories drawn,
The hidden truths, secrets of the dawn.

Chasing Sunbeams

Through open fields where wildflowers sway,
We chase the light of breaking day.
In golden streams, where sunbeams play,
A dance of joy, in morning's ray.

Laughter echoes through the trees,
Carried softly on the breeze.
In sunlit paths, our spirits rise,
Chasing dreams beneath the skies.

Reflections in the water bright,
Moments caught in morning light.
Each step we take, a timeless quest,
For sunlight sought, we give our best.

Boundless fields and skies so blue,
Each ray of light, a guide anew.
In every shadow, light we find,
Chasing sunbeams, hearts aligned.

As day unfolds, the journey's kept,
In every ray, our hopes are swept.
Chasing sunbeams, through it all,
In light's embrace, we stand tall.

Wanderlust Skies

Beneath the canvas, azure spread,
Where dreams and whispers softly tread,
I wander paths the starlight paints,
Embracing hues the dusk acquaints.

Each cloud a ship that sails so free,
To distant lands, across the sea,
A journey beckons, hearts to claim,
In skies where no two days are same.

Through endless skies my spirit flies,
Chasing where the horizon lies,
With each sunrise, a tale unmasked,
Of voyages that hearts have tasked.

The winds of wonder lift my sails,
Beyond the valleys, through the dales,
Where secrets kept in whispering trees,
Are carried forth on gentle breeze.

A wanderer's heart, forever torn,
Between the dusk and golden morn,
In skies of dreams and boundless seas,
My soul is wind, forever free.

Beyond the Twilight

As twilight fades, the night unfolds,
A tapestry of starry golds,
The mysteries of worlds unseen,
In silent whispers softly dream.

The moonlight bathes the earth below,
In silver streams, a gentle glow,
A realm where shadows come alive,
And ancient stories still survive.

Beyond the edge of evening's grace,
In realms where time's a still embrace,
The past and future gently meet,
In rhythms of the heart's own beat.

Each star a tale, a fervent wish,
In night's vast ocean, dreams who swish,
A dance of light in cosmic sea,
Where endless night holds mystery.

In twilight's wake, the heart does soar,
Through boundless dreams of evermore,
For in the night, the soul finds light,
Beyond the shadowed veil of night.

Silhouettes in the Distance

Against the setting sun, they stand,
In quiet grace, with shadows grand,
The silhouettes in twilight's hue,
With tales that time itself bestrew.

The past etched in each silent form,
Through summer's heat and winter's storm,
They whisper secrets to the night,
In fading glow of twilight's light.

Beneath the moon's soft tender gaze,
They turn to phantoms in the haze,
A dance of shadows, calm and slow,
In twilight's gentle afterglow.

Each figure holds a world within,
Of joy and sorrow, loss and kin,
A silent watch through time's expanse,
In silhouettes' eternal dance.

In dusk's embrace, a tranquil song,
Of shadows where our dreams belong,
The silhouettes, a timeless lore,
In distance faint, forevermore.

Ethereal Ends

Where earthly bounds begin to fade,
And dreams in vivid colors wade,
The ethereal meets endless skies,
In realms where unseen beauty lies.

A world beyond our mortal ken,
With visions rare and gentle then,
In whispers of the stars aligned,
Through cosmic dance, our fates entwined.

The veils of light in twilight's grasp,
Where hope and love in shadows clasp,
An endless dawn, no end in sight,
In ethereal realms of glowing light.

A journey to where dreams ascend,
In timeless winds, our souls defend,
The place where earthly ends dissolve,
And all our truths and myths evolve.

In silent awe, we stand, embrace,
The ethereal, a boundless grace,
Beyond the ends, where dreams unbind,
In timeless flow of cosmic mind.